Rust or Go Missing

CLEVELAND STATE UNIVERSITY POETRY CENTER
NEW POETRY
Michael Dumanis, Series Editor

John Bradley, *You Don't Know What You Don't Know*
Lily Brown, *Rust or Go Missing*
Elyse Fenton, *Clamor*
Emily Kendal Frey, *The Grief Performance*
Dora Malech, *Say So*
Shane McCrae, *Mule*
Helena Mesa, *Horse Dance Underwater*
Phillip Metres, *To See the Earth*
Zach Savich, *The Firestorm*
Sandra Simonds, *Mother Was a Tragic Girl*
Mathias Svalina, *Destruction Myth*
Allison Titus, *Sum of Every Lost Ship*
Liz Waldner, *Trust*
Allison Benis White, *Self-Portrait with Crayon*

For a complete listing of titles please visit
www.csuohio.edu/poetrycenter

Rust or Go Missing

poems

Lily Brown

Cleveland State University Poetry Center
Cleveland, Ohio

Copyright © 2011 by Lily Brown

All rights reserved
Printed in the United States of America
Printed on acid-free paper

ISBN 978-1-880834-91-6

First edition

5 4 3 2 1

This book is published by
Cleveland State University Poetry Center,
2121 Euclid Avenue, Cleveland, Ohio 44115-2214.
www.csuohio.edu/poetrycenter and is distributed by
SPD /Small Press Distribution, Inc. www.spdbooks.org

Cover image: Cy Twombly; Untitled Part I, 1988 [Rome];
Oil, water-based paint, graphite, and metallic paint on wood
panel with painted frame; 75 ¼ x 42 ¾ inches; Cy Twombly
Gallery, The Menil Collection, Houston, gift of the artist;
Hickey-Robertson, Houston. © Cy Twombly. Used with
permission of The Menil Collection

Rust or Go Missing was designed and typeset by Amy Freels
in Optima with Stone Print display.

LIBRARY OF CONGRESS CATALOGING-IN-PUBLICATION DATA

Brown, Lily, 1981–
 Rust or go missing : poems / Lily Brown. — 1st ed.
  p. cm. — (New poetry)
 ISBN 978-1-880834-91-6 (alk. paper)
 I. Title. II. Series.

PS3602.R722283R87 2010
811'.6—DC22

2010023933

Acknowledgments

Grateful acknowledgment is made to the editors of the following journals in which poems from this collection have appeared:

Back Room Live:	"Poem Starting with a Comment Written on a Poem"
Boog City:	"Sitting in the Car"
Coconut:	"Its Character"
	"Old with You"
	"With Music"
Cannibal:	"In the Shins"
	"Noon's Compartment"
Denver Quarterly:	"History"
Fence:	"The Return to Radical Innocence"
Handsome:	"Knower"
	"The News"
Left Facing Bird:	"Morning. The Poem Is Dead"
	"New Yorker"
Lo-Ball:	"Backpedaling for Statements"
	"Sensed" (as "Poem")
Octopus:	"Rust or Go Missing" (as "This Backwards")
	"To Left from Right"
	"Transference"
	"Water-Rocking"
Parthenon West:	"Museum Armor"
Pleiades:	"Leaf at the End"
	"The Phosphorescent Dark"
	"Tropicalia"
Shampoo:	"Smaller Gulls Before"

So and So: "Smoking Through Green and Smoking Blue"
Tarpaulin Sky: "Dead Animal Machine"
Typo: "To a Tree"

"I Name" was published as a limited edition broadside by the Rope-a-Dope Collective, in conjunction with the So and So Series. "Ex-Sonnet" was published as a limited edition broadside by Nikkita Cohoon, in conjunction with the Kalamazoo Book Arts Center. "Smoking Through Green and Smoking Blue" was published as a limited edition broadside in conjunction with The So and So Series. "To Left from Right" and "Leaf at the End" were republished as poem-films by Joshua Marie Wilkinson for *Rabbit Light Movies*.

Poems from this collection appeared in the chapbooks *The Renaissance Sheet* (Octopus Books), *Old with You* (Kitchen Press), and *Museum Armor* (Doublecross Press). Thank you Mathias Svalina, Zachary Schomburg, Justin Marks, and MC Hyland.

Thanks to my teachers, without whom I wouldn't write poems. Thank you Doug, for setting me on this path and for friendship. Thank you to my teachers at Saint Mary's: Graham Foust, Brenda Hillman, Norma Cole, Michael Palmer, and Chris Sindt. Thanks to all of my classmates at Saint Mary's. Thank you Adam Watkins, Andrew Kenower, Brett Fletcher Lauer, Hazel McClure, Maricela Ramirez, Mike Sikkema, and Sharon Osmond. Thank you to Claire Becker, poet friend and inspiration. Additional thanks to Graham for help with these poems, and for teaching renunciation. Thank you to everyone at Cleveland State University Poetry Center. Thank you to Joe Massey and Ed Pavlic for comments on some of these poems. Thank you Joshua. Thank you to my sister, Rebecca. This book is also dedicated to my grandmother, Katherine Andler Swartz.

to my parents

Contents

Backpedaling for Statements	5
Smoking Through Green and Smoking Blue	7
Ex-Sonnet	8
With Music	9
Sitting in the Car	11
To a Tree	12
Transference	13
First Position	14
Its Character	15
Smaller Gulls Before	17
What Was Cannot Be Taken	18
Rust or Go Missing	19
The Return to Radical Innocence	21
Old with You	25
Knower	27
Leaf at the End	28
In the Shins	29
Family or Places	31
Water-Rocking	32
Dead Animal Machine	33
Poem Starting with a Comment Written on a Poem	35
On Reading	36
Sensed	37
Nobody Is in Cahoots with the Telephone Pole	38
Noon's Compartment	39
Cloud on Mountain	40
Morning. The Poem Is Dead.	41
To Left from Right	42

The News	44
Experience	45
Kinetics	46
The Eaten	47
I Name	48
New Yorker	49
Greeny	50
Dirty Movie	52
The Phosphorescent Dark	53
Tropicalia	57
History	59
The Matter	60
Museum Armor	61

Rust or Go Missing

"My imagination was a tarnished mirror."
NATHANIEL HAWTHORNE

*"There are not leaves enough to crown,
to cover, to crown, to cover—let it go—"*
WALLACE STEVENS

Backpedaling for Statements

She says the book can't feel the smart
of tumble and hit. But here, in the office,
window cases mini-landscape. Window cut
by brown rulers, run through and across
the grass. Now a world—impression
of groundcover and tree with sunlight.
She says the book can't feel
but I'm inside. The book has many
minds. She wants to know the climate
of the room where I last wrote.
Was it the living room? Was it the staircase,
the memory of a staircase? I make a lie
of the absolute, space like a reflection
that never changes. And it's space
she's after. Space where she has me build
statements out of ignorance. Here are
the words. Here is a length, a pause,
a glance out the window
for effect. Here is the way I heard
toads in the woods, walked without
paths in the woods, saw a golden
golf course through the woods
and sneaking to the greens found everything
was wrong. Fake fountains in the watery parts.
Oh god, in the restaurant we overhang
the ocean, overhand the ocean, underlie
erosion. There's music in the dining room

and people at the window. A motor
in the lot. China clucks the table
and what's it made of? Milk?
Milk? Because it holds milk. For felines?
For children? Because it's white?
Did you see that dog? That dog?
That dog head out the window. Oh god,
you've confirmed the voices, the moonlight
through the boulders off the coast. Strange
paths cut through boulders. Last night the moon
so ruddy we couldn't confirm it.
The sayings we know. The warnings
we've heard about moons and sailors.

Smoking Through Green and Smoking Blue

I'm like the window, painted
white, a manufacturer of squared

light. To mold, with one's hands,
the cliff fog, I use my eye. Time's

quartered; the physical progress is
in the sky. Pelicans drop their

hinges, planes on the sea, planing
the sea. Over there, on another

blue piece, green fringe hangs.
The day's back darkens.

Ex-Sonnet

All my life, I saw the same
people. New freckles. Brown

moons. I don't know, pinions,
skin. Arms hung on the train

strut. Animal, animal
in the tree's

beam, I see you standing
in your cradle.

With Music

I work to my eye. Bird body
to my right.

Creaky-winged white pelican—change
my life, live fossil,
plaster mower with music.

A woman tells a pregnant woman
she dreams her stomach's
ripped out.

What the kid listens to in there.

Mother, don't worry about the missing
phone calls. You're worth more than
vacillation, all I've heard.

The singer said he hears the city
with no alarms or cars.

The song unreal
and true. Pigeons shit on anything.

One August, an hour out of the city,
the light lost it.

What was an electric
keyboard is a horn.

Give the power outage.

The plastic poem owns
you, brain.

Sitting in the Car

Swallows fall from
wire, silver tributes

to the sun—who comes
here? Deer-faced cows

in the open range.
The black bird tucks

her wings. Swallows
all from wire. We

pass. Sideways, we are
bodies; one dimension,

being moved.

To a Tree

Eucalyptus is the object, it means

project. Bathe in its leaves. Sob its oddity

to the sidewalk. Defend its non-nativity.

Take on the tree and fistfight

desire. Shadows lie. I see them:

features, limbs, ink with shifty

edges. Break it atypically, the day

to pieces, each differently

visible. Shade open so the street

is lined. Evening tree is salty

with dusk. Early sun distributes

risk. Its lineage casts shadows,

shadows that pull a tree down.

Broken, legible heap.

Transference

I am watching TV. We expect too much
from each other. Our faces are made
of stairs. Each step hardens.
Each case concludes nothing.
I am floating
down the stairs
after a morning
of serial drama. Fantasy
plays its part; TV weds me
to reverie. A sailboat's a vessel.
A sailboat's on the stair.
I've let you box my insides.

First Position

In the library, as much quiet
as you can fit in your head.

I walked across a giant stone and
bloodied my knees on the way up.

There's another giant stone, one I
can't climb. I take the sleeper train

through an old-fashioned intersection
near the Florida-Georgia border.

Everyone waves to me. White book
with blue circles. Blue book with white

circles. Paper pile bound in black.
Hands emboss the library's walls.

It's dark again, in the between-finger
spaces. I'm done and the thoughts are

gone. This isn't the greatest time.
All around me voices sell their sinkables.

I separate the one from the one.

Its Character

This could be a photo of wood, black ink
scored across it. The cracks are real.
No, wood's plied into a shape.

Remove the paper.
Green spine meets black
face in a lifted ridge.

We've restored the original,
one-poem-per-page model. The original?
I face the wall. My back to the dead-bug

curtains and their tale of white.
I'm elsewhere. Sounds let up at the top
and fade. I have a radiator full of water.

It could be bad for my health, everything
with plugs, unidentified in the hedge.
Authentic stamps on the floor. I turn across

the bed. I need shelves, I need storage. I need
to stop who you are. In the fantasy
head, you always write. It happened that one p.m.

passed and she signed her letters with one word,
then five words, then three words, then six.
Unroll your quarters-in-paper, poem

in a bad time. I'm in the wilds without
my feet. In the slick cedar swamp,
all is a primitive green. The lightless thicket

where even the air's hung up
and colored, the tree line sticks the clouds.

Smaller Gulls Before

I want the tree a mile up to shake
its blond leaves to the pavement.

From my plot I think it odd that birds
don't shit on us more often.
We're right here ruining the sand.

I too further the obesity of gulls.
For years I've let them steal
my sandwiches and sealing wax.

That with which we stamp our selves
we stamp with our selves.
Sink of emblem in that wax.
Lies that swap stories with heart.

What Was Cannot Be Taken

The blue jay near
the trail is tense
and blows apart.

Brown spot above
his tail, below
his wings, mumbles.

He won't work for blue jay.

The blue bird is blessed
with ignorance.
Night words are lost by day.

Rust or Go Missing

I think the plastics
and sink them. Rock, snow globe, buffalo nickel

collection, this or that
amalgamation of shiny unrecyclable shit.

The sun on the dirty river's mug was better.
At the high window

someone's face was stronger.
The letters, non-silicone, nonpermanent,

an invisible anchor on sea floor,
under a boat I've never seen,

reflect like a watch face on the ceiling.

•

In January the hills
unbutton their pants,

ward back the swept-up winter,
eastern plow's attempt to file.

Here, west of it, hill with cleft-chin climbs, big
with water-busting leaves, above the freeway.

Tree posing as flower:
make the machine mistaken.

⦁

A woman talks quietly.
It's her nature.

A man talks loudly.
It's his nature.

Have they chosen each other or is it fiction,
what they see?

Through his eyes, through hers, light may bounce
specifically from their features.

I can't see light sneaking

anywhere. He says, *while you enjoy your coffee,
I'll go to the bathroom.*

He says, *here's the light. I place it in your glass.
Here's how light stays when I'm gone.*

The Return to Radical Innocence

A stopwatch measures held breath.

- •

Stagnant communions roll us tight with worry.
Steam engines have no unconscious
so they do what comes. What comes naturally
with us is in hiding, is just hiding.

Wanting light and buying hammers.

- •

Television teaches top and bottom.
She thought she saw the future
in a square and let the new life pass.

The skin trade was not new.
She had it on the inside. Silence
is an outer skin—neither crab grass
nor sand collar has a voice.

Touch sand and dirt.
See them new in the trees.

- •

The man hears what he wants.
In another language

communication tilts.
I don't know the word for *back*
so I say *eleven* and *please*.
He takes eleven, gives me nine.

•

In the book, the last sentence circles
on siblings. Those who know
in a singular knowledge.
Like no one else. Like no one else
with whom we trade words.

•

Feeling doesn't change:
cartoons are dreams, memories
are better and worse.

The edges of these stairs are inexact,
like a supinator's sole.

•

There's a girl with a girl belly in my eye.
Perfect is less
sweat, a slower heartbeat.

The choice between old and new
room. Is it perfect being always new.

•

The spreading of the renaissance sheet
over thought is a good mood. A good noon.

It's the letting and teeth
showing.

The sheet comes and goes
without lines.

- •

Let navigates
the room alone.

The sincerity hasn't struck.
The sheet isn't specific.

- •

The renaissance sheet is an entrance.
Sound is the real
room, whether forest or house, it's the dead
flowers on the floor and their fragments

when touched. The sheet lifts to let sound
onto the ground. It crawls a hedge,
tries to escape what comes
naturally, lands tangled in ash.

- •

Resisting silence
is like resisting breath.

•

There's fascination and joy around interruptions
in public places, around knowing
people listen in.

•

The teeth are out after.

Old with You

I wait for my wrist lines.

If I push them,

boxes make themselves.

∙

I shorten your name
to a letter to make
you new.

Time spreads.

These materials
populate my life.
Cursors in mud.

I turn on the weather.

The weather
ashes the books.

The house can live
underwater. The house
can wear its rooms out.

So what if the house.

The primitive is a process
more real, more hated.

Real book, the thoughts
in you are secondhand.

Knower

I don't miss out on what
I miss. You were right
about the future, a feeling
attached to now. Here,
my trick: accompaniment.
Trade the images for new stock.
You, lagging between too-close
and too-far. First I was alone,
waiting. Then I was alone,
alone.

Leaf at the End

I climbed a giant leaf at the end
of my imagination. Across
the spotted water, the hill
fastened its yellow bushels.

The imagination asked for all the cities,
for the canopy to get its machines out
and tile the leaves. My friend Lily
assumes what I want and it's so unfair.

The imagination shoves in and pushes
blithely out, a belt of pelicans, a plank
of hard clouds, bunches of doorknobs
halo the street-blighted hills.

I find a pile of antlers in the woods, assembled
for burning. I crawl beneath them and stay
there when the burners come with their fire.
Up in the canopy I dangle, touching nothing.

In the Shins

Nothing means like a poem means
to court me, like a poem means
like burnt wood to flake off.

Comic books, electronics, shitty
substitutions for love. Shifty things
break off of me like a field

of turning hands, all waving goodbye.
Goodbye, cave. Goodbye, simulacrum.
Hello, ether. Hello, sorry,

I lost the footing. Even language pivots.
I address myself to the boats.
How buoyant the kingfisher, stuck

as it is near the ocean. In the new
dark, cats squeal certain questions.
Their mouths like jagged diamonds.

Well-mannered needles in black bags.
The neighbors and I kiss the doorjambs.
Somewhere between a place and a family

an arc of pins makes shadow
of the masses. Of the masses waving
in the museum, of dotted architecture

and the masses trembling through the floor
in the museum. The man in the shop
brandishes a ream of staples on paper.

Exchange of hands. Arm-shaped
mirror. What consciousness
stands; we close our eyes but I know

we're breathing. If my arms make
a cross. If our arms make a cross.
There are stones stacked up the sky.

In their grass the foolish bugs.
Now we're stung.
The swelter's up—we love privately

and consciousness bears loving
out. Brittle shadow. The hill bent me.
Sheets nudge and crease and burn.

Sheets aren't places. Sheets aren't
family or places.

Family or Places

The nightclub is huge. The bouncer
lets a flower in. You stumble
out of your face.

The shrub says Affirmative
and Negative. A man presses
his arm up to the wind.

Pistils in the yard, pistils all
over the apartment die
and handle my fingers.

A man or a woman rolls his
or her head back in
the peopled auditorium.

A child croons
Woah in the green place, hovers
to kite on hill's horizon.

Our time and its pictures
are unrecognizable. Oh, look at that
bad page tearing itself.

Water-Rocking

A big red boat with blue
trim floats, some water
slams against a rock.
Far away, another rock splits.
The top half shoves the sand.
Children lose. Bears slip
from ice. The kid with the horse
on his car drinks beer
and crushes the can; he takes three
parking spots to parallel the ocean.

Dead Animal Machine

Speech fathers the weak.
Paper floor. Plaits of paper
in my hair. Hand parleys the pelt-
laden pavement.

(We install pelts under streets and leave
a window for transparency's sake.

And for the children.
All new zoos are underground).

Hands in hysterics. We clack together.

We ride out on volcanic fields. Steam rises
orange from black pastures. I'm not
for antagonizing the gods and we worry

for the gods. Loose rocks and leaf tearing.
Boats scare dolphins and what a view
the gods enjoy, buried in the moon-

basin hills. Boats in the shapes of circles, dusk
loving sharks. I choose a thing for its surface,

its dark reflections. I wake messy. I wake
lacking eyes. Then I'm animate again.

The trees' tresses blow

into the sun, shards of speech
revolutions, of tonal informants.

I want social, want ears.

Poem Starting with a Comment Written on a Poem

It's awful, we carry it with us.

An entire lexicon that subsists

only in mattresses.

The way phrases bring about spit

repeatedly, repeatedly

kick down the mountains, curl

their toes. Stamina winks.

The tunnel is a stem

between angry, slinky

cars and speed. Their turning over

corrodes the mouth.

On Reading

I was working
on my speech
when the shower
head said, Speak
man. The sickness
said, You thought
to make speech
less devastating and this is
punishment.
What is hand
written with spindly
tails won't touch
the rim. Thought
works off its mooring.

Sensed

I separate. Try to
in the speech act.
How successful.
Hair flouts head.
Bones disclose the skeleton
when feet unflex. The uncontrolled
must be restricted. The air
pinned up like a bride
before a crowd. Each face
wears a mask of adult faces,
adult water from adult
showers, adult smiles sensed
through the telephone.
The ceiling with its stars.
I'm not having one kind
of experience. The ocean
at once inaudible and flat,
hot and thick with weeds.
A tree dies alone,
wounded up the trunk.
As if compression.
As if amputation.
We might keep the tree
and this the first, world I love.
The air untacks the sea.
The sea is coming inside.

Nobody Is in Cahoots with the Telephone Pole

I eye the sill, watch water
seep under windows
and doors, cover furniture,
rest softly upon mantel.
I see a hurricane's innards,
want the ocean to overflow.
I wish I flooded daily.
Outside my window men
and women scream.
Why must every twosome
become a jigsaw,
watertight? Where is the chord
of flies that wailed past me?
We don't speak. No one believes
one thing follows another:
the path between sun stalk
slicing wall
and wintered pavement
is deeply broken.
Sense this and I'll love you.
I turn into full sight.
There is no body.

Noon's Compartment

By the river, staid, long
cords of bone.

Thin boats slid by.
We heard the sound
of dressed-up humans.

Fancy boats, inchoate moods
in noon's compartment.

Afterwards, we walked
the sand and our shadows
knocked hard and froze.

Red light, purple light
behind Highway One,
you are only so

beautiful in the sun burned
eye, in the under-lid's grit.

Two circles brush fire
on the palm.

Cloud on Mountain

Cows with both ears
tagged. The pragmatist
ventures a guess.
Man with poem
in eye sallies
into my face. Each
meeting is new,
each glance corners
different. One stigma's
a cursing, hoof-hurry away.
Uncertainty's a tattoo
not in my skin.

Morning. The Poem Is Dead.

I should take scissors to it,
step skeleton from body, by the hand.
In the hovel of dreams things
touch me and won't.
Sheets litter the knees.
Sun slips down a piece of wall.
The lamp's soft shade
thins, pales. The light
develops and it's like this
every morning. I wake with a body
in the sheets. It stains
the eye blacker for the light.

To Left from Right

Lift up and enter the body
from above. Be the window

that lowers to wall,
in houses on bays,

where glasses are ships. Sink

by sleight of water
and not by wreck.

•

Conversation's cobbled
from complaint. When none remain

I am a case complete. The difference between people
and drakes is we paint ourselves.

•

Waves are greyhounds
that out-shoulder one another.
The seal's not stopped. Surface

breaching is more than we manage.

•

I found the secret—

Don't tell
him what he sees. We can't see

from his mammalian eyes.

There's one question.
The name we'll give

it's an apparition.

- •

The seal's whiskers sense something

above and to the side.

- •

When I say *we* I don't mean
we're the same. I mean

we fall on each other.

The News

Embarrassed by the contents
of the mouth, the filing
and its forms, one fights to keep
from telling teeth and ruckus.

We use autos for artillery.
The way white diminishes,
costumes are the faithful
and graveyards pound down.

The bug stalls
along the cheek.
Dear sediment. Dear
collateral. Dear traces.

Experience

I copy my hands
to look through them. Expose

my insides! I scream
at the lyric maker and everyone

in their quadrangle cars. I want
to know who sees me drop

hair from the window
I open only a hint.

Kinetics

Train-pressed
air absorbs me.
The past halved,

silvered, done-down.
The mirrorless
image its proof.

I learn from
the refrigerator,
a bottle moved

from under
my hand. Slow
motion sticks.

The Eaten

Staring at each
other through screens,
we participate.

Insane, the way
the profile views
you, the eaten

grows an eye.
The eaten spits
up happiness.

There's a state for
each watchfully
foiled part.

I Name

something something,
to understand. A
temporary piece.
Thought, images
repeat. I skim
for feeling, no
literal intent.

New Yorker

This cover makes the pigeon

look pretty, psychedelic

even, its skinny purple

legs and crowbar feet

above the crowbar streets.

Greeny

It feels weird just standing so I put my foot
against the other leg and stand until I wobble.
The sun sets early. The light days fly.
Some nights, we watch the sun set over
the water but behind the point.
We photograph constantly. Sameness
and landmarks are terrifying. Color
we run out the kitchen door for. No flash,
but color seeps longer, darkens yearly.

All the walls fall when the head hears
the nightmare. How easy to be giddy:
when faced with nightmare, stare it down.
How lucky to unfix eyeshine from shapely
mind, things functioning.
When striating ribbons of white sand
make strips so small,
morning clarifies.
Prepare to face sunlight with little
or no sunscreen. No dark glasses.

We become obsolete, not or else.
At the edge a turquoise line extends.
It's painting, but pretend
it's something else. At the edge
tundra green bumps sky purple
bumps sand bumps ocean grey

bumps red, fiery red above. At the edge
we walk. Pale interstices. Waves deafen
and flatten. Be honest. In the painting,
there are mountains.

Dirty Movie

They're nudes this way.
Lithe-limbed hard bodies,
of confident cockatiel,
of fearless sparrow.
Their lying down
on their backs
on the white
grassland is sufficient.
If they sleep fitfully,
my own albino kindling
eddies some water, emits
dreams of worn teeth,
white powder.

The field acquiescing
beneath the wind
is no longer not a sheet.
The kind without
springs at its corners.

The Phosphorescent Dark

I

Fascinated, I stay in
for days, riding cars

straight through stop
signs, riding cars past

speed signs that blaze
white, head-

light shining back
penalty. This is

about the busted
date, getting lost

in the couch; all the
genies that fill

the phosphorescent dark.

II

Where is the sand-
man hiding the dirt.

III

I have three lives in
three closets. To build light

in them, you stand up inside.
I sat on the floor of the first,

admiring my sills. I
struck the mirror, pounded

in the door and had a vision.
Name, stomach,

and a voice, and in the tiny space
that made their middle, that made

a middle, I was the slackest place.

IV

From the book, I've a vision
of the future seen clearly in

a vision of the future.
In that place the mind

went, it gave itself away.

Tropicalia

I lost the book. Could we find the book, together
again, outside the patch of tropicalia, emerge

together, morning of January 2nd, unsullied?
I'm touching walls. It means something.

My furtive relationship to birds. I saw you
on a field of mud and the mud was important.

Derived from a shady hall; prior to memorization,
I had squares of light. Position of body

on back. In bed before dark, I saw rabbits
out the window. Tell them I'll come for them.

Tell them we saw them in our dreams, fed them
carrots and white clover and they liked it.

That my teeth are talking. That teeth of light
kept me up late summer nights.

Information in the dark. Dendrites in the body
and dendrites in minerals look like trees.

Proof that one night bends the mouth,
day the eye. On the long, tanned path

we write without hands. Greenery
and imagery bending in all directions

away from the sun. This enlarges the spine.
I know the spine. I know I'm not the spine.

History

Birds heel the sky I
see through the body
scamming the mind.

Briefly not alone, then
not alone, I work hard
to rearrange the sand

when I do wrong.
The table's flat tone,
my pony Christmas hope.

Beneath the microscope
we see donuts, soap,
tree bark chipped apart.

The Matter

Night dims. Low fire
inks it, fire written

by the pamphlet we read.
I see you beside, a blind

on the night. On the cold
side, tree seeds beat

cut wood. You walk
from structure, your outline

on the door, the matter
of you moving.

Museum Armor

A fishtailed woman
mounted my wall, gave

me a feeling. I thought
of nuns. The clock flashed

on the ceiling; time was
inside. I found you

under the owl-white
sky. I scratched the glass

with my eye. Tipped birds
over the red bridge.

The sun in my wall.
We slant. Speech

centers our backs.

WEST ORANGE PUBLIC LIBRARY
3307800486723 7

```
811.6 BRO
Brown, Lily, 1981-
Rust or go missing : poems
```